A HOLIDAY BOOK

New Year's Day

BY LYNN GROH

ILLUSTRATED BY LEONARD SHORTALL

GARRARD PUBLISHING COMPANY
CHAMPAIGN, ILLINOIS

Especially for Nancy

Holiday Books are edited under
the educational supervision of

Charles E. Johnson, Ed.D.
Associate Professor of Education
University of Illinois

J
394.2
G

Contents

1

The Year's Birthday

Everyone loves a party. There is one party that everyone attends: the birthday party for the new year!

New Year is a holiday all over the world. Bells ring, whistles blow and horns blare. People parade in gay costumes. They sing special songs and eat special foods.

5

Everyone celebrates New Year—but not everyone celebrates on the same date. That is because people measure time in different ways.

In some parts of the world, people measure time by the seasons. For some, spring is the beginning of the new year. For others the old year ends when crops are harvested. These people hold a New Year festival in the autumn.

Some people celebrate New Year's Day on the shortest day of the year, or the winter solstice. That comes just before our Christmas, on December 22. Others celebrate on the longest day, which is June 21, the summer solstice.

In the South Pacific, there are island people who have a new year every few months. The weather there is always warm. Farmers plant crops all through

the year. Every time they plant a new crop, the people celebrate a new year!

Still other people measure time by the coming of the full moon. An American Indian, for instance, would not say that something happened "many months ago." He would say, "many moons ago."

In the United States, however, and in most modern nations, time is measured by the sun. The earth goes around the sun in a great circle. It takes 365¼ days to go all the way around. So our year usually has 365 days. Every four years, on Leap Year, an extra day is added at the end of February. This takes care of the extra quarter days.

Our New Year's Day is January 1. That date was chosen by the Romans about 2,000 years ago!

No matter when it is, New Year has the same meaning everywhere. It means that an old period of time has passed, and a new one is beginning.

It is a time of hope for a brighter future. Most of all, New Year is a time of fun.

2
How It Began

No one knows just when the custom of celebrating the New Year began. It was thousands of years ago.

People then lived by hunting and by farming. They measured time by seasons. Spring was the season to plant seeds. There were greens and berries to eat. Crops grew fast during the warm summer. In the autumn, the crops were harvested. These were good seasons.

Then winter came. Nothing grew in the fields and the people had little to eat. The days became shorter, the nights longer. The people shivered with cold. They were frightened for they knew very little about the world. They feared the sun had gone away and might never return.

Of course, the sun always did return. The earth was warmed and turned green again. How happy the people were! At the first sign of green, they celebrated New Year.

Our word "year" comes from an old word that meant "springtime."

In the old days, men believed in many gods. Some believed their gods gave them a new year as a gift. The year might be good or bad. Or there might be no new year at all! It depended on whether or not the gods were happy.

The New Year celebration was then a religious festival. The people did many things to make the gods happy.

Often the celebration began with a parade. Someone beat on a drum or a gong. People sang hymns as they marched. Sometimes the parade led to the banks of a river. Flowers and other gifts were thrown into the river. These were for the gods of water.

Some people paraded into the fields to honor the gods of the crops. Still others went to a special place in the forest, or on top of a hill.

Usually there were altars in these special places. The people prayed and sang songs of praise. They left gifts on the altars for the gods. Among these were fruits, grain, flowers and animals. The animals were killed and burned in a solemn ceremony.

The people also burned incense. They thought the pleasant smell would put the gods in a good mood.

Then a feast was prepared for the gods. The food had to be very special to be "fit for a god." A calf or a sheep might be roasted. Often special cakes were made with honey.

The people joined in eating the feast. "Breaking bread," or eating together, was a solemn ceremony which bound the people to each other. Since the people believed their gods were present, the feast also bound them to their gods.

The New Year festival usually lasted several days. Then the people went to plant their crops. Now, they believed, the gods would give them another year.

And the gods always did!

3

The Chamber of Fates

New Year was celebrated in Babylon more than 4,000 years ago. Babylon was a city in Mesopotamia, in Asia. It lies between the Tigris and Euphrates Rivers. Today this land is called Iraq.

Marduk was the god of Babylon. The Babylonians believed Marduk had made the world and everything in it.

14

They also believed there were monsters who wanted to destroy the world. Marduk had to fight the monsters every winter. If Marduk should lose, there would be no new year.

The Babylonians eagerly watched for spring. When it finally came, they believed Marduk had won the battle. There was a great New Year celebration. It lasted eleven days.

During the celebration, everything was done backward. Masters changed places with their slaves. There was a great feast when slaves sat at the table. Their masters waited on them.

One of the slaves was chosen king to rule for five days. He lived in the king's palace and wore the king's clothes. He could have anything he wanted.

After five days, the slave-king was

15

killed. The real king returned to his throne. Now, the new year could begin in an orderly way.

The Babylonians believed the evils of the past year had to be washed away, so the new year could start clean. They washed themselves in a special ceremony. They put on new clothes.

The high priest bathed in the waters where the Tigris and Euphrates Rivers run together. The Babylonians believed this water was sacred.

The priest carried some of the sacred water to the great temple of Marduk. His helpers sprinkled it about inside the temple. They beat on bronze kettle-drums. The noise was meant to drive out evil spirits.

When Marduk's temple was clean, priests came to Babylon from other cities in Mesopotamia. They brought statues of their gods with them. Each city had its own god. Because Babylon was the chief city, people believed Marduk was the chief god.

The statues of all the gods, including Marduk, were taken to the temple. They were put in a room called the Chamber of Fates. The people believed the gods read the record of each person for the past year. Then they decided the fate, or future, of the world for the new year.

The people wondered what their fate would be. They made many resolutions, promising themselves to do better the next year. While they waited, they had a gay carnival. They wanted to have fun while they could, just in case the new year would not be a happy one.

Later, the gods were taken in chariots to the Euphrates River. They were put

on a boat called the "New Year House" and were entertained.

All the boats on the river were decorated with flowers and ribbons. Special plays were put on. The actors wore masks, which stood for good spirits and evil spirits. The good always overcame the evil.

That was what the Babylonians hoped would happen in the new year!

4
A God with Two Faces

New Year in ancient Egypt started with a flood!

The Nile River floods every year. For the Egyptians, the flood is a great gift. Their land is dry and it almost never rains in the summer. Without water from the flood, their crops would die.

The flood was so important that the Egyptians started their New Year when it began. This was in June when Sirius, the

Dog Star, is seen at dawn. The Dog Star is the brightest star in the heavens. The Egyptian New Year festival lasted five days and five nights.

One night was called "The Night of the Drop." The Egyptians believed that a magic drop of water, falling into the Nile, started the flood. On the "Night of the Drop," they read signs to tell the future.

A lump of dough for each member of the family was put on the doorstep. If the lump cracked during the night, the owner would have a long life. If it did not crack, the owner would have bad luck all year.

The Egyptians were good astronomers. They were the first people to have a sun year of 365 days like we have today.

Across the Mediterranean Sea from Egypt was Greece, in southern Europe.

Greece was divided into city-states. Each city-state had its own calendar. None of the calendars was alike. So the Greeks had many different New Year's days. Each celebration honored one of the many Greek gods.

Dionysus was the god of fields and vineyards. The Greeks believed he died every winter and was born again every spring. In the spring, farmers put a figure of the baby god in a basket. They carried it to the fields so Dionysus could bless the crops. As the crops grew, Dionysus grew older.

The crops were harvested and the grapes were made into wine. In late December the people had a feast for Dionysus. There were religious dances and songs which told the story of his life. At the end of the festival Dionysus, now an old man, died.

Kronos was the Greek god of Time. Kronos decided how long all things should live. He gave years, and he also took them away. His feast day was on the winter solstice, December 22, the shortest day of the year.

The Romans lived in southern Europe too. They fought the Greeks and conquered them.

The Romans learned many things from the Greeks. They even "borrowed" some of the Greek gods. One of these was Kronos, but the Romans changed his name to Saturn. His festival was named Saturnalia. It began about December 17 and ended on the winter solstice. There was much feasting and merrymaking. Even slaves were free to do as they pleased. This festival became the Roman New Year.

The Romans had a calendar but it was not accurate. Sometimes the calendar said it was winter, when it was really spring! The calendar was always being changed.

Julius Caesar became an important Roman leader. He decided his people needed a new calendar that would not change. A Greek scientist named Sosigenes helped him invent one.

Sosigenes went to teachers in Egypt.

They taught him how to measure the sun year of 365 days.

The old Roman calendar had ten months. Sosigenes added two more months to make twelve in all. This rhyme tells how many days he put in each month:

Thirty days hath September,
April, June and November;
All the rest have thirty-one,
Excepting February alone,
Which has just four and twenty-four,
'Til Leap Year gives it one day more.

Today, 2,000 years later, we still use the Roman calendar! The Romans also named our months. Many of them were named for Roman gods. January was named for the Roman god Janus, who ruled over gates and doors. Statues of Janus had two faces. He could see people either entering or leaving the gates.

Caesar made January the first month of
the year. The Romans thought Janus
would be able to look back at the Old
Year, and ahead to the New Year.

Janus had twelve altars, one for each
month. On the first of January, the
Romans built great fires on each altar.
The fires burned for the whole month.
Priests made offerings to Janus on each
altar every day.

The Romans believed in magic and omens, or signs. On New Year's Day, they went to seers, or fortune-tellers. They believed the seers could read the future in the stars and in other signs.

They believed that what they did on New Year's Day would bring them good or bad luck for the year. They were careful to be especially nice. They visited their friends and gave each other presents. They settled quarrels with their neighbors.

All workers did some labor. Farmers plowed a furrow in their fields. Housewives did some chores. This was to make sure they would keep working all year.

Great feasts were held. People often ate and drank too much. There were many wild, rowdy parties.

That is how New Year's Day was kept when the calendar was new!

5
New Year in Europe

"Prosit Neujahr!" say the Germans.
"Bonne année!" say the French.
And the Spanish say, "Feliz año nuevo!"
They all mean, "Happy New Year!"

There are many languages spoken in Europe. But there is only one New Year's Day. That is because Rome became a great empire. Roman armies captured most of Europe and the British Isles. Caesar's calendar was taken to every country.

Roman customs were spread everywhere. However, people in the captured countries kept some of their own customs too. Slowly the customs mixed. There came to be many ways of celebrating New Year. Most of them were as rowdy as the Roman holiday.

Then the new Christian religion spread. The Christians would not celebrate the rowdy Roman holiday. Instead, they went to church on January 1. January 1 was the start of their year for legal and government matters. But they held a second New Year festival in the spring. March 25 was the Christian New Year. Finally, in 1582, Europeans changed the Christian New Year to January 1. But England did not change until 1752, only 200 years ago!

People like holidays to be gay. Most Europeans went back to the Roman idea of parties and games at New Year.

The celebration came to have two important days. December 31, or New Year's Eve, was celebrated as the last day of the old year. People said farewell to the old and made ready to welcome the new.

Midnight is the moment when the old year ends. In most countries people still wait up until midnight to see the new year in.

In one German city, people open their windows when it is nearly midnight. As the clock begins to strike, they lean out

and all shout at once, "Happy New Year!"
What a loud cry it is!

In England, many people still open their
front doors at midnight to let the new
year come in.

In Roman times, people in Scotland
believed the first person to enter one's
home on New Year's Day was very
important. If the person was a dark man,
it meant good luck. If a fair man entered
first, he brought bad luck. It was a sign
of very bad luck if any woman entered
the house first.

32

Some families hired a dark man to come to their home. He was called a "first-footer." He waited at the door until midnight. Then he was sure to be the "first foot" to step inside. Many Scots still play the first-footing game, but it is all in fun now.

Scottish children also play a game on New Year's Eve. In Scotland, December 31 is called "Hogmanay," but no one remembers what this old word means.

The children wrap themselves in sheets. They fold part of the sheet in front to make a big bag. Then they go from house to house, singing:

> *Hogmanay, Trollolay,*
> *Give us of your white bread,*
> *And none of your gray!*

They are given special New Year cakes, also called hogmanay.

33

French children receive gifts at New Year's instead of at Christmas. Children in Belgium also get presents, but only after they play a trick on their elders.

The children find keys to all the rooms in the house. They watch for a chance to lock some grownup inside a room. The grownup must promise to pay a ransom before the children will unlock the door.

Long ago, there was a belief that the

old year would not leave by itself. It had to be driven away! There were many ways to do this. In many countries these things are still done for fun.

In Hungary, the old year is "burned out" with great bonfires. In Germany, Greece and some other countries, it is "cracked out" with whips.

A favorite way to drive away the old year is to make loud noises. Firecrackers,

horns, drums, tin pans—anything that is very noisy will do. The noise also drives away evil spirits.

The happiest New Year sound of all is the ringing of bells. These lines by a famous English poet named Alfred, Lord Tennyson, tell of the bells at midnight:

Ring out the old, ring in the new,
Ring, happy bells, across the snow:
The year is going, let him go;
Ring out the false, ring in the true.

6
Iroquois Jubilee

New Year was celebrated in America long before the white man came. American Indians had a New Year too.

The Iroquois Indians called their festival the "New Year's Jubilee." The Jubilee was held about the first day of February, depending on the moon. It lasted seven days.

The Jubilee was announced by two "Keepers of the Faith." These men were religious leaders.

The Keepers of the Faith dressed in bearskins. The skins were fastened on their heads with cornhusk wreaths. The men wore cornhusk bracelets and anklets. Their faces were painted.

They went to every house in the village. Everyone had to be told that it was New Year. Each family was told the rules for the Jubilee.

Houses were scrubbed and cleaned. Rubbish was burned.

Evil spirits were driven out. This was done by burning tobacco as incense.

Each person made peace with his enemies. All arguments had to be settled or forgotten. No one was to be angry during the Jubilee.

Everyone was to take part in the ceremonies. Only the sick were excused.

No one was to mourn during the Jubilee.

If someone died, the body was to be kept in the snow. The funeral would be held when the Jubilee ended. Then the whole village would weep with the family.

Prayers to the Great Spirit were said in each house. All the family took part. They asked forgiveness for sins of the past year. They gave thanks for their blessings. Then they asked the Great Spirit to send a good new year.

On the second day, all the families visited each other. Each person carried a small, new shovel. In each house, each visitor went to the fireplace. He stirred the ashes with the special shovel. Then he picked up some ashes and sprinkled them on the hearth. He said a prayer: "I thank the Great Spirit that he has spared your lives again to witness this New Year's ceremony."

He took another shovel of ashes. He sprinkled these on the hearth, saying: "I thank the Great Spirit that he has spared my life again to be an actor in this ceremony. I do this to please the Great Spirit."

The visiting went on all day from sunrise to sunset.

Next there was dancing. This was done mostly by the younger men and women. The dances had a religious meaning. They were like prayers that were acted out instead of being spoken.

The dancers were divided into groups. Each group had a different dance. One group might do the Feather Dance. Another chose the Fish Dance. Still another would do the Trotting Dance. Each group danced in every house. The dancing went on for two days!

Young boys liked to do the War Dance. They dressed as warriors like their fathers. They danced just as their fathers did before going to war.

The most important event of the Jubilee was the White Dog Ceremony. The dog was killed on the first day of the Jubilee. Red spots were painted on it. The dog was decorated with colored feathers. Each feather stood for a prayer.

The dog was placed on a pole in a place of honor in the village. The Iroquois believed that the dog's spirit stayed with the body. The spirit watched all the Jubilee ceremonies. It heard all the prayers of the people.

On the fifth day of the Jubilee, a great altar was built. A fire was lighted. All the people of the village paraded to the altar. They marched around it chanting hymns.

The Keepers of the Faith put the white dog on the fire. The people prayed aloud as it burned.

The Iroquois believed that the spirit of the dog came out of the body in the smoke. The smoke carried the dog's spirit to heaven. The dog's spirit had heard all of their prayers. It would give their messages to the Great Spirit. Then, they believed, the dog's spirit would live with the Great Spirit forever after.

43

The Iroquois had special New Year games. The "Thieving Game" was for children. The children went in groups from house to house. With each group went a grandmother. She carried a big basket. At each house the children received gifts, which were put in the basket.

If the children liked the gift they danced to say "Thank you." Sometimes they did not like the gift. Then they would try to steal something from the house. If they were caught, they had to give back what was stolen. If they were not caught, they could keep it.

At the end of the game there was a feast for the children. There were more games and dancing. The whole village also had a feast at the end of the Jubilee. The main dish was made of corn and beans. Today we call this dish "succotash."

7
Old Ways in a New Land

The Europeans who settled in America brought their New Year customs with them. What a rich collection of customs it was!

The Pilgrims and the Puritans who settled New England did not celebrate at all. They believed it was wrong to keep a holiday that honored the pagan god Janus. They called January "First Month."

The Dutch settlers who lived in "Nieuw Amsterdam" liked to have fun. They held open house on New Year's Day. The men called on all the families they knew. The ladies served holiday foods and drinks.

When the English came, they changed Nieuw Amsterdam to New York. But they kept the custom of open house. They served fancy foods such as pickled oysters and boned turkey. Imported chocolate and rare wines were also served.

Eggnog was a favorite drink. It is made of eggs, milk and spices. In some parts of England, it was the New Year's "wassail bowl." The word "wassail" comes from a very old word that meant "good health." Before drinking, guests lifted their glasses and said, "Wassail!" Or they might say, "To your good health!" We call this ceremony a toast.

In those days, children were "seen and not heard." They ate the New Year's goodies, but the celebration was for the grownups.

Older children did go to church on New Year's Eve. Many churches held services called Watch Night at which people kept watch for the new year. Before midnight the bells rang a sad farewell to the old year. Then as the hour struck, the bells rang out a merry welcome to the new year. The people sang a hymn or said a special prayer. Watch Night is still held in many churches in America.

Some settlers in Pennsylvania came from Moravia. That was a small country in Europe which is now part of Czechoslovakia. During their Watch Night service they welcomed the new year with a band of trombones! Then they had a "love feast"

of coffee and special cake, as a sign of
friendship and brotherhood.

The Swedes, who settled in Maryland,
ate ham for good luck on New Year's Day.
The Germans in Pennsylvania ate herring,
which was supposed to bring riches in the
new year.

When America became a free nation,
New Year remained the same. Even the
first President, George Washington, held
open house. Members of Congress called
on the President. So did ambassadors
from other countries. Private citizens were
welcomed too. Mrs. Washington served
special punch and cake.

The week from Christmas to New Year
was one long winter holiday. Gay parties
were held every evening in the cities. The
biggest party was on New Year's Eve.

Great banquets were served, then there was dancing. At midnight the guests drank many toasts to their friends and to the new year.

In the country, people lived far apart so there were few parties. Still, most families stayed up to see the new year in. Often gifts were given on New Year's Day. The oldest son might be given a farm of his own or a team of horses. Girls were given dishes or linens for their "hope chests." A hope chest was filled with things a girl would need when she got married.

Everyone made New Year's resolutions. Children often wrote their resolutions on paper and put them on the wall above their beds. Then they would be reminded of their good resolutions every night of the new year!

51

8
Moon Year in America

Some Americans still celebrate a New Year that is measured by the moon. The Jews and the Chinese have a "Moon Year." Some American Indians celebrate as their ancestors did.

No one knows exactly when the Jewish New Year was first celebrated. It was at least 3,000 years before the Romans invented our calendar.

The Jewish celebration is held in the autumn, around the middle of September. On New Year's Eve, there is a family feast. The table is decorated with fruit. Special foods include bread baked in round, smooth loaves. It represents the wish for a smooth new year. An apple dipped in honey is eaten so the new year will be sweet.

It is a solemn but happy feast. The family reads special psalms and stories of Jewish history from the Old Testament.

New Year's Day is known as Rosh Hashanah, or "Day of Judgment." The Jews believe that God judges all people on this day, according to their deeds of the past year. The "Ten Days of Penitence" follow. During this period, the people can atone for their wrongs through prayer and good deeds.

The days of penitence end with Yom Kippur, or "Day of Atonement." On that day, God is believed to write down the fate of each person. The Jewish New Year greeting is, "Leshanah tobah tikkatheb."

"May you be written down for a good year!"

Chinese people live in many parts of the United States. Such large groups of them live in San Francisco and New York City that both cities have sections called Chinatown. The Chinese New Year comes in February. It is so gay that many visitors go to see the fun.

The festival lasts for fifteen days, beginning with New Year's Eve. That evening there is a family feast. No one leaves the house and no visitors can come in. Everyone stays up until the new year arrives at midnight.

During the following days, the Chinese visit their friends. There are special games for children. People get ready for the Feast of the Full Moon. This is also called the Feast of Lanterns and comes on the last night of the festival. Brightly colored paper lanterns appear in windows, doorways and along the streets.

On the Night of the Full Moon, men, women and children gather for a big parade. Their costumes are as bright as the lighted lantern that each person carries.

Most colorful of all is the giant dragon which leads the parade. It is made of bamboo sticks covered with paper or silk of many colors. Men and boys get under the dragon to carry it.

The parade goes slowly down the street. Watchers cheer and set off loud fire-crackers. Sometimes people tease the dragon. Then he dashes toward them as if to bite! It is all in fun. The dragon is the Chinese symbol of goodness and strength. He leads their parade into a good new year.

9
Our New Year Today

In the 19th century people in America kept moving westward. They took their customs with them. Some customs changed because of different ways of living.

Across the South there were great cotton and tobacco plantations. People lived far apart. When they did visit, they usually stayed several days in the big plantation homes. House parties were popular at New Year's time. Big feasts were served. There was dancing and merrymaking on New Year's Eve.

Later people went to the Southwest where there were big cattle ranches. Lonely cowboys went to the nearest town to celebrate New Year. They had noisy, wild parties in saloons and dance halls. At midnight, crowds of cowboys went into the streets and shot their guns to welcome the new year.

In California, New Year's Day was celebrated like the Fourth of July. The flag was raised. Patriotic speeches were made. The people shot off firecrackers. Often they ended the celebration by parading noisily through the streets. Later the parades were better planned. One of them, started in 1890, is still held today. That is the Tournament of Roses, a parade held in Pasadena.

All through the nineteenth century, America kept growing. In the big cities,

59

New Year was celebrated like an old Roman carnival.

Some wealthy people rented ballrooms in big hotels. They entertained their guests with fancy foods and drinks from Europe. Champagne came from France. It is still a favorite New Year drink.

Gypsy fortune-tellers read the future for the guests. They gazed into crystal balls. Or they read signs made by tea leaves in the bottom of a teacup.

There was music and dancing. Often the guests wore gay costumes and masks.

Masquerade parties are still popular today. People dress up to represent a famous person or a god of olden times. A favorite is Father Time. That comes from Kronos, the Greek god of Time. He is an old man, dressed in flowing robes. He carries a scythe for reaping the years.

Another is the New Year Baby. He is dressed only in a diaper and wears a funny hat. He comes from the Greek god Dionysus, who was born new every year. There are pictures of Father Time and the New Year Baby on New Year cards.

In New York City, people began the custom of gathering in Times Square to welcome the new year. Today, thousands of people go there to watch the clock atop the Times Building. When its hands point to midnight, a great cheer goes up. There is a din of noise from bells and horns. People shower each other with paper confetti, which is a symbol of good wishes.

Today, there are still New Year's Eve parties at hotels and clubs and restaurants. But many people prefer to have small, quiet parties at home. On New Year's Day, families often have open house.

The holidays are a time to put aside work and school to enjoy the company of friends. We do the same things that have been done since ancient times.

We make New Year resolutions, because we know we have to do better things to

have happier lives. We meet our friends to show that we treasure them. We eat and drink together as a sign of fellowship. We sing songs together.

One favorite New Year song honors old friends and the old year. At New Year's Eve parties, people link arms as they sing:

Should auld acquaintance be forgot,
And never brought to mind?
Should auld acquaintance be forgot,
And days of auld lang syne?

Auld Lang Syne was written about 200 years ago by a Scottish poet, Robert Burns. It means "old long-since" or time that has gone by. "Auld acquaintance" are old friends.

We welcome the New Year with these happy words:

For he's a jolly good fellow,
Which nobody can deny!

64

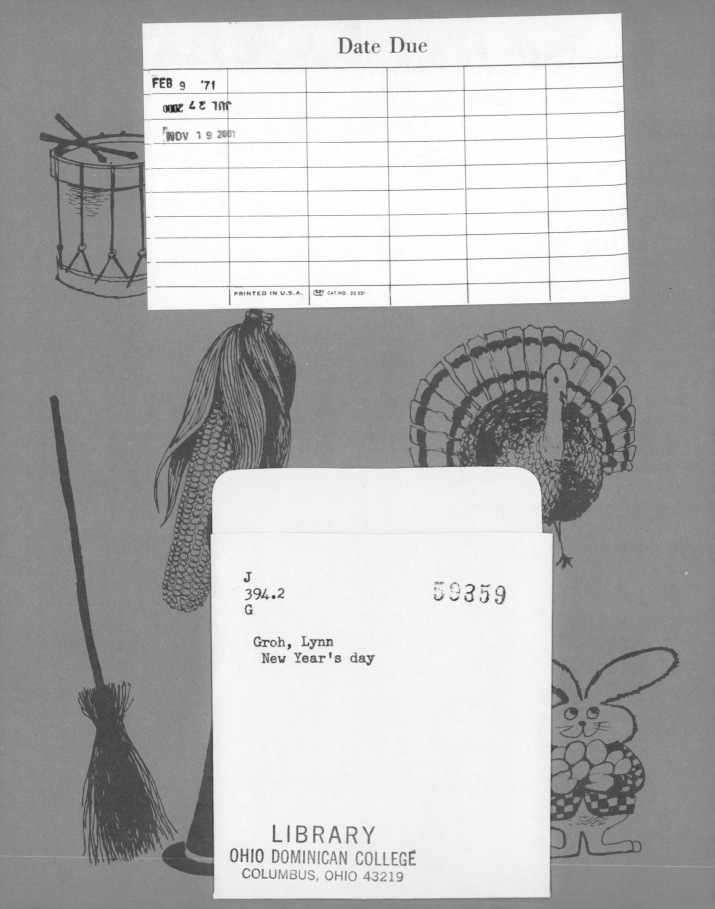